FARGO PUBLIC LIBRARY

Dealing with Challenges

Bullying

By Meg Gaertner

www.littlebluehousebooks.com

Copyright © 2022 by Little Blue House, Mendota Heights, MN 55120. All rights reserved. No part of this book may be reproduced or utilized in any form or by any means without written permission from the publisher.

Little Blue House is distributed by North Star Editions:
sales@northstareditions.com | 888-417-0195

Produced for Little Blue House by Red Line Editorial.

Photographs ©: Shutterstock Images, cover, 4 (top), 4 (bottom), 6–7, 9, 11 (top), 15, 19, 20–21, 22, 24 (top left), 24 (top right), 24 (bottom right); iStockphoto, 11 (bottom), 12, 16–17, 24 (bottom left)

Library of Congress Control Number: 2021916789

ISBN
978-1-64619-482-7 (hardcover)
978-1-64619-509-1 (paperback)
978-1-64619-561-9 (ebook pdf)
978-1-64619-536-7 (hosted ebook)

Printed in the United States of America
Mankato, MN
012022

About the Author

Meg Gaertner enjoys reading, writing, dancing, and being outside. She lives in Minnesota.

Table of Contents

Bullying **5**

Dealing with Bullies **13**

Being Kind **23**

Glossary **24**

Index **24**

bus

playground

Bullying

Bullying can happen anywhere.

It can happen at school or on the bus.

It can happen on the playground.

Bullies make others feel unsafe.

They might push or trip others.

They might take others' things.

Bullies make others feel bad.

They might say mean things.

They might make fun of others.

Bullies make others feel alone.
They might leave others out of a group.
They might pick on people in front of others.

group

Dealing with Bullies

Being bullied can hurt.

But do not bully back.

Instead, be kind and firm.

The bully wants your attention.

But you do not have to give it.

Act like you do not hear the bully.

Or just walk away.

The bully wants you to feel alone.

But you are not alone.

You can stay with a friend.

You can stay in a group.

The bully wants you to be angry or unhappy.

Instead, stand tall and be brave.

Take a deep breath.

Then tell the bully to stop.

The bully might keep bullying.

If so, tell an adult.

Bullying is wrong.

The adult can help.

Being Kind

You might see someone else being bullied.

If so, you can be a good friend.

Be kind to the person.

Everyone has the right to feel safe.

Glossary

bus

group

friends

playground

Index

A
adult, 20

F
friend, 16, 23

K
kind, 13, 23

S
safe, 23

24